A Trip to the Zoo

by Joanna Lake

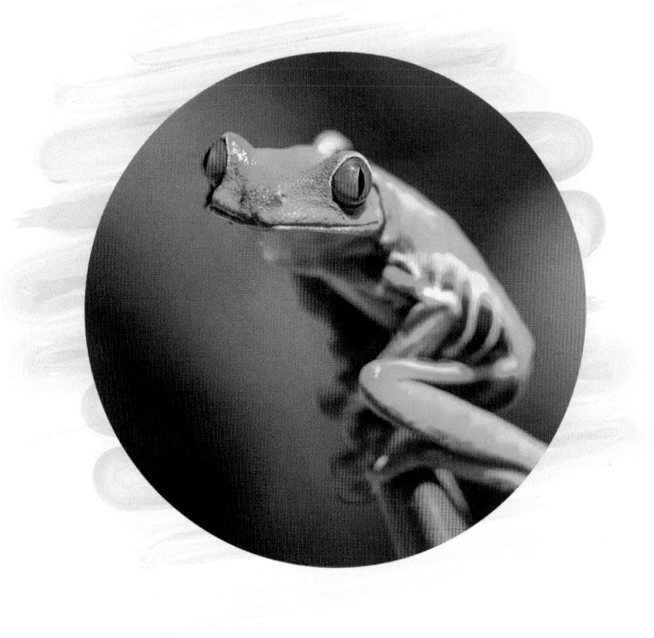

OXFORD
UNIVERSITY PRESS
AUSTRALIA & NEW ZEALAND

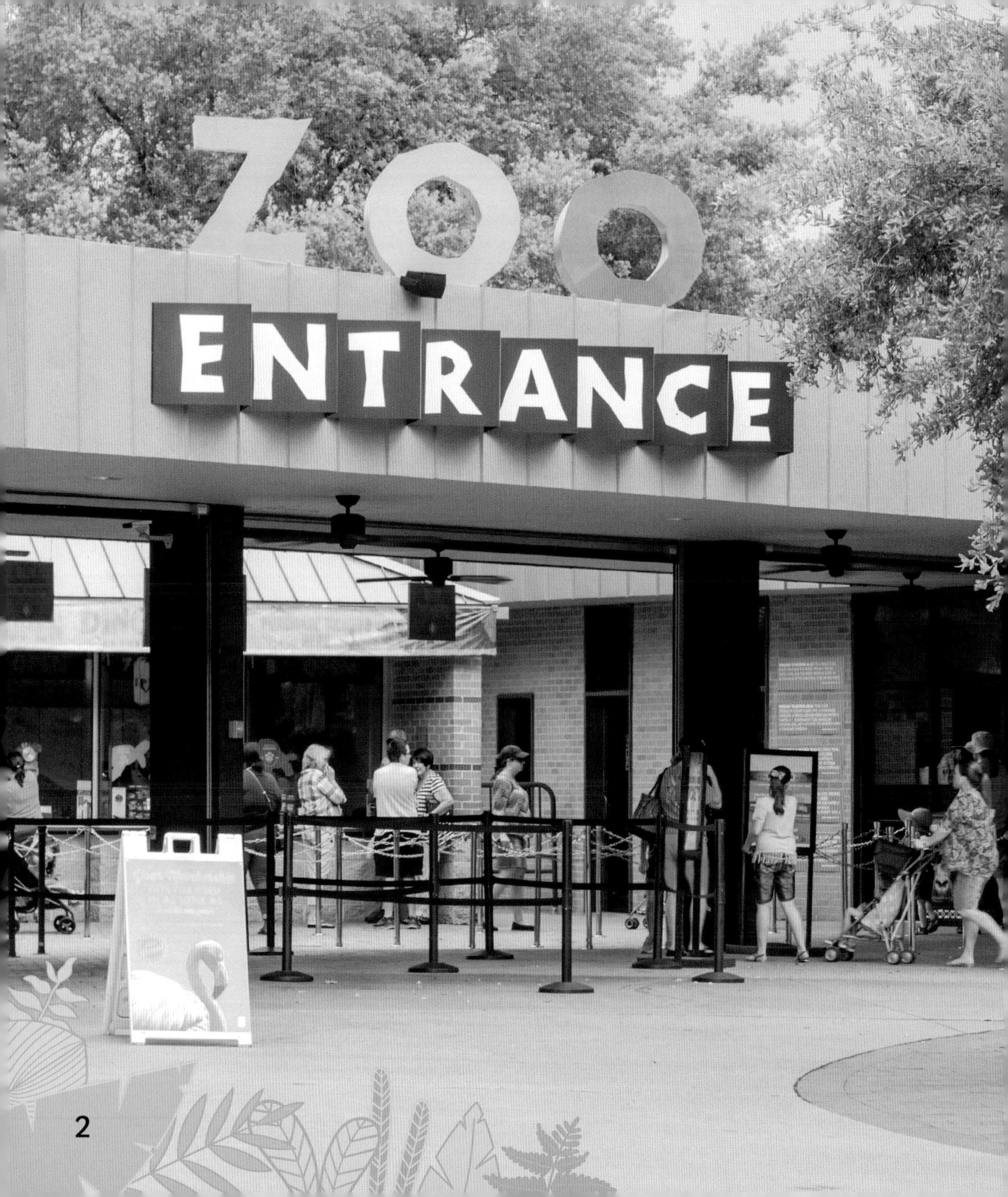
ZOO
ENTRANCE

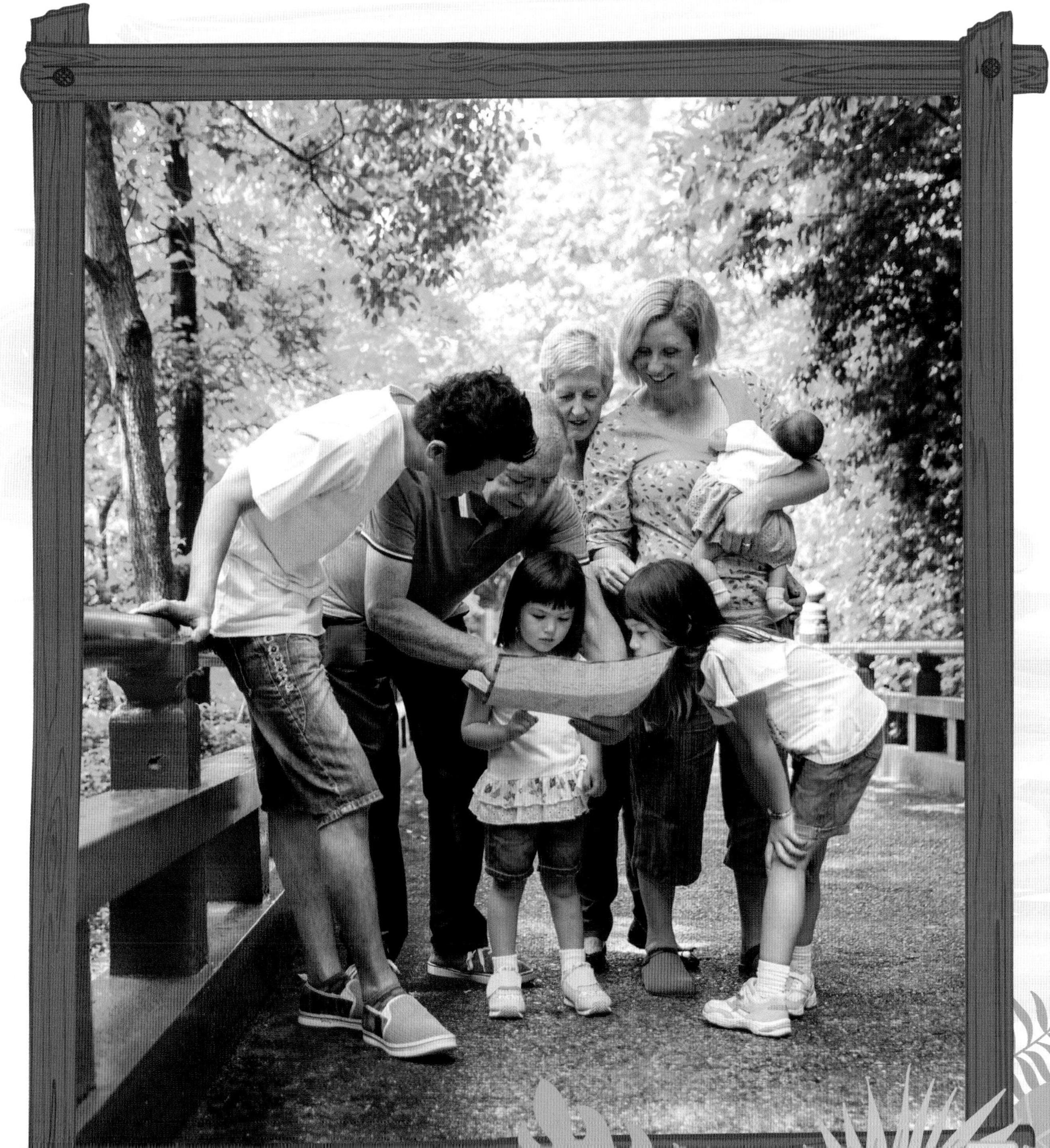

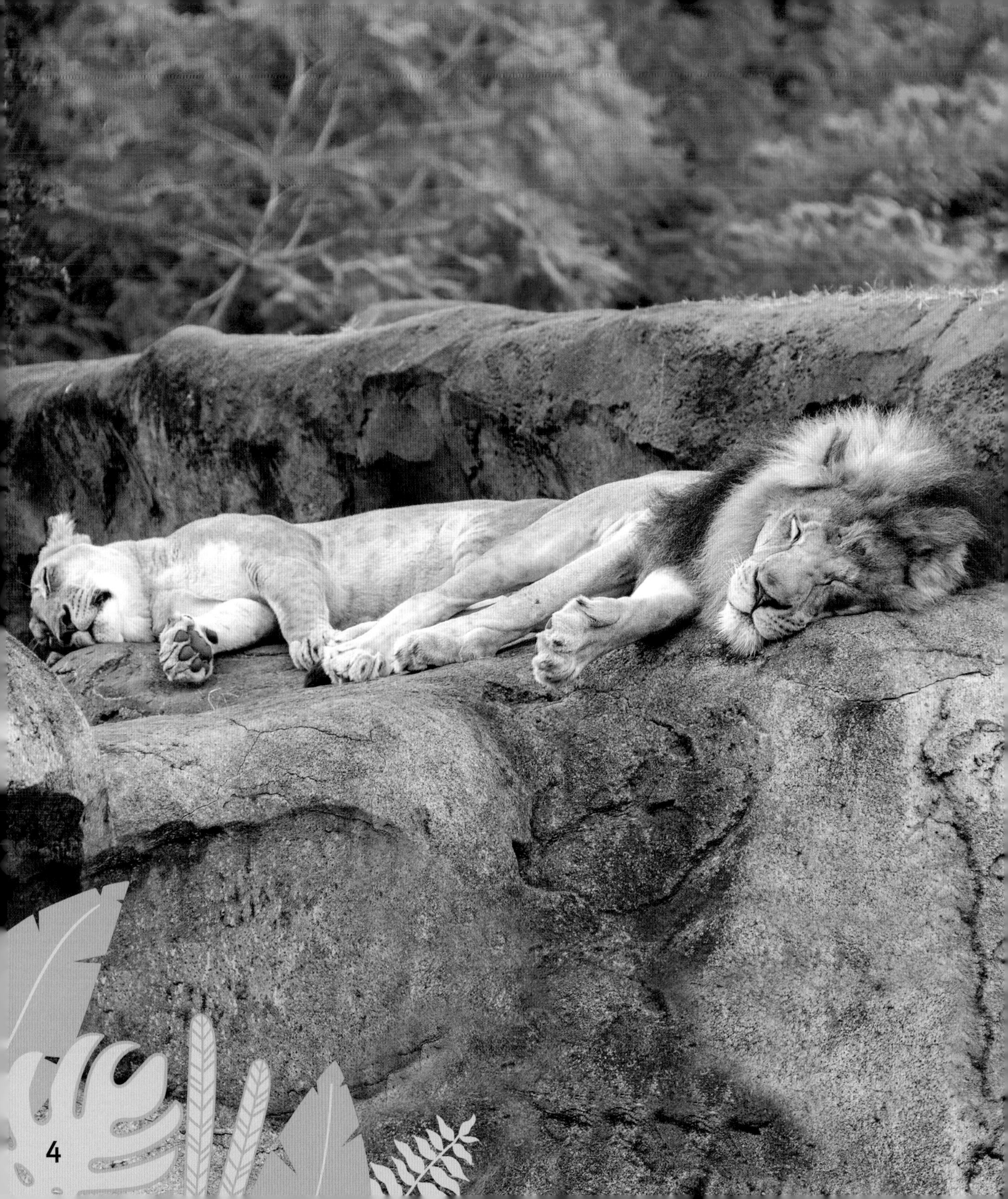

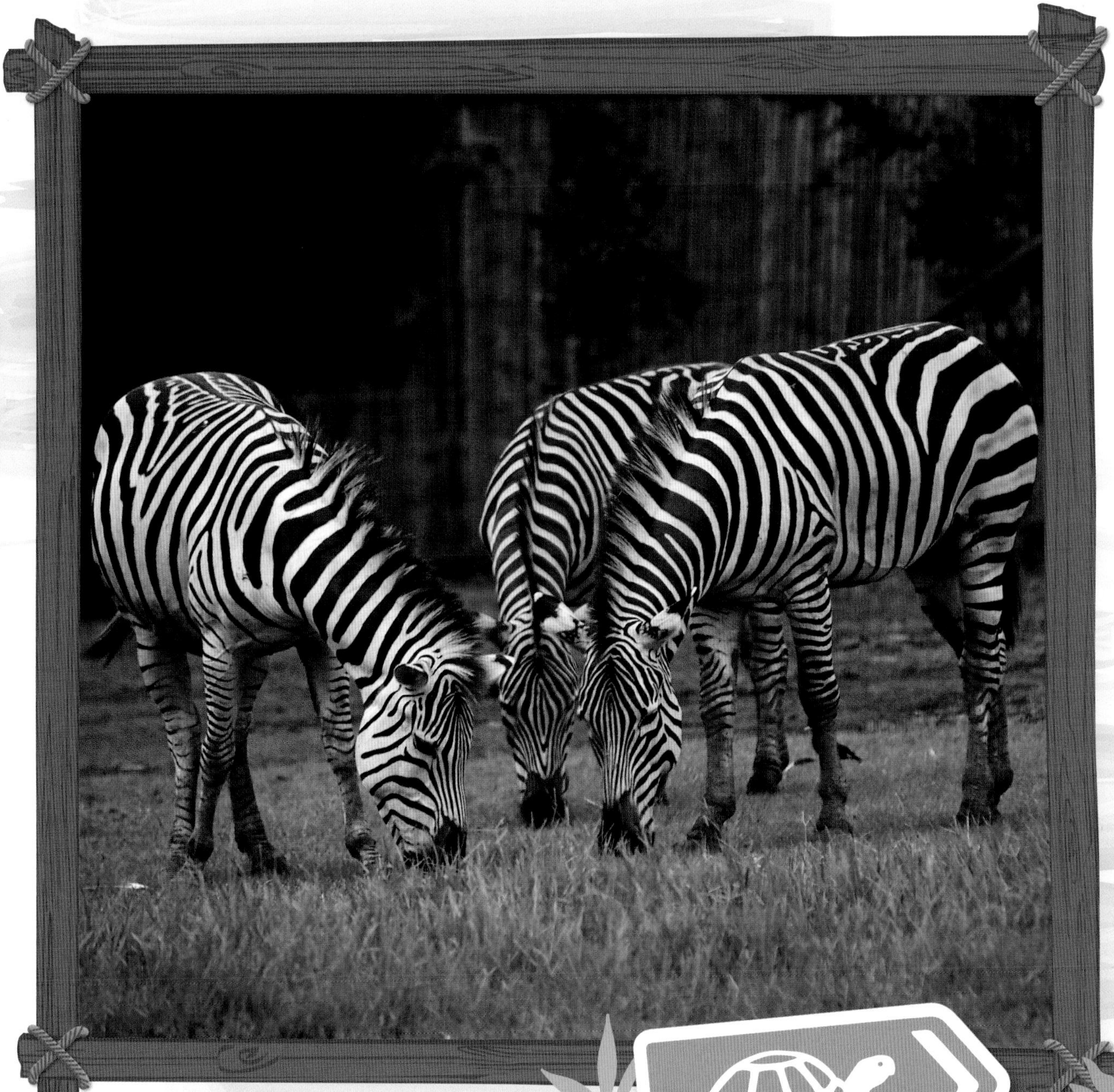

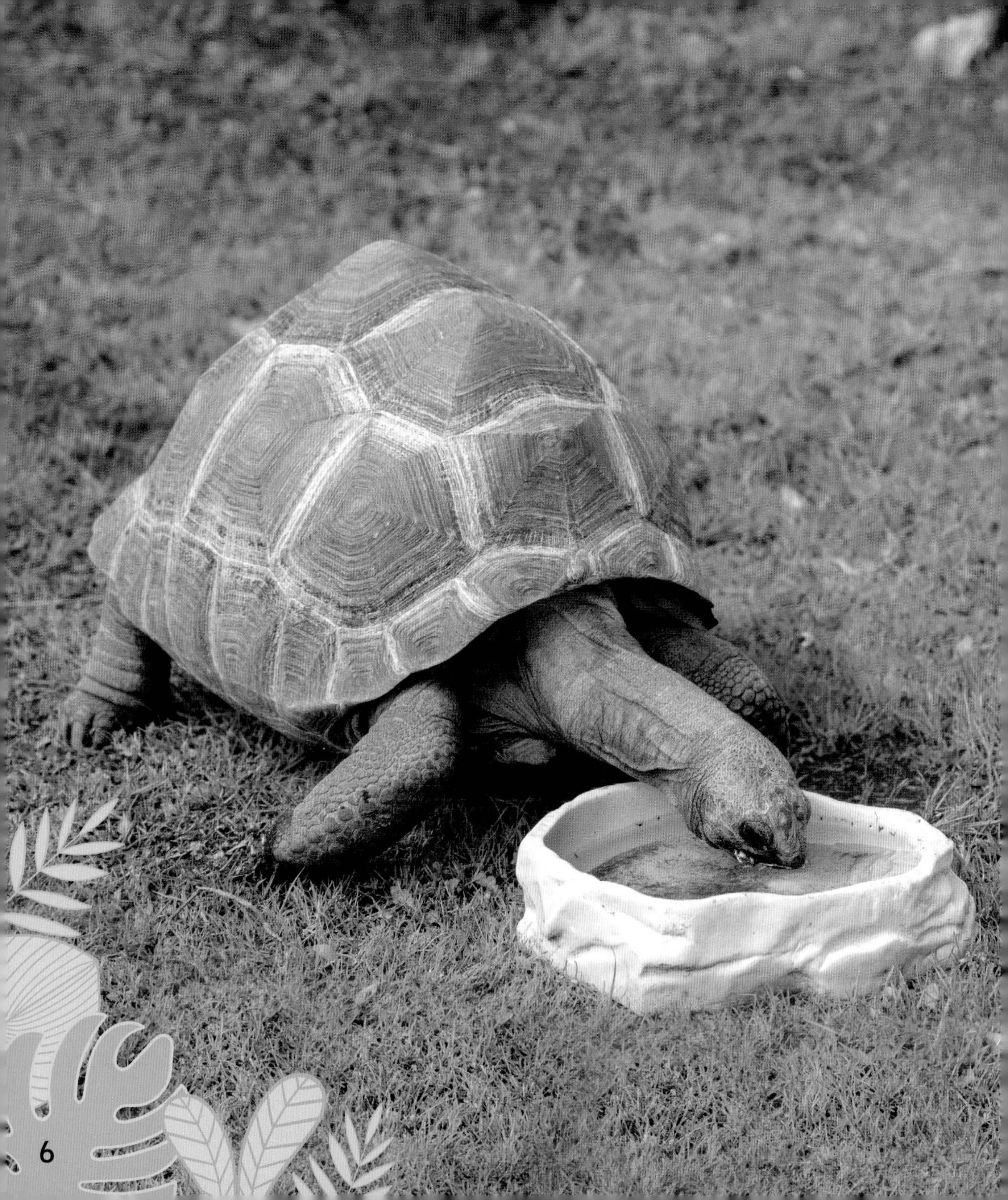

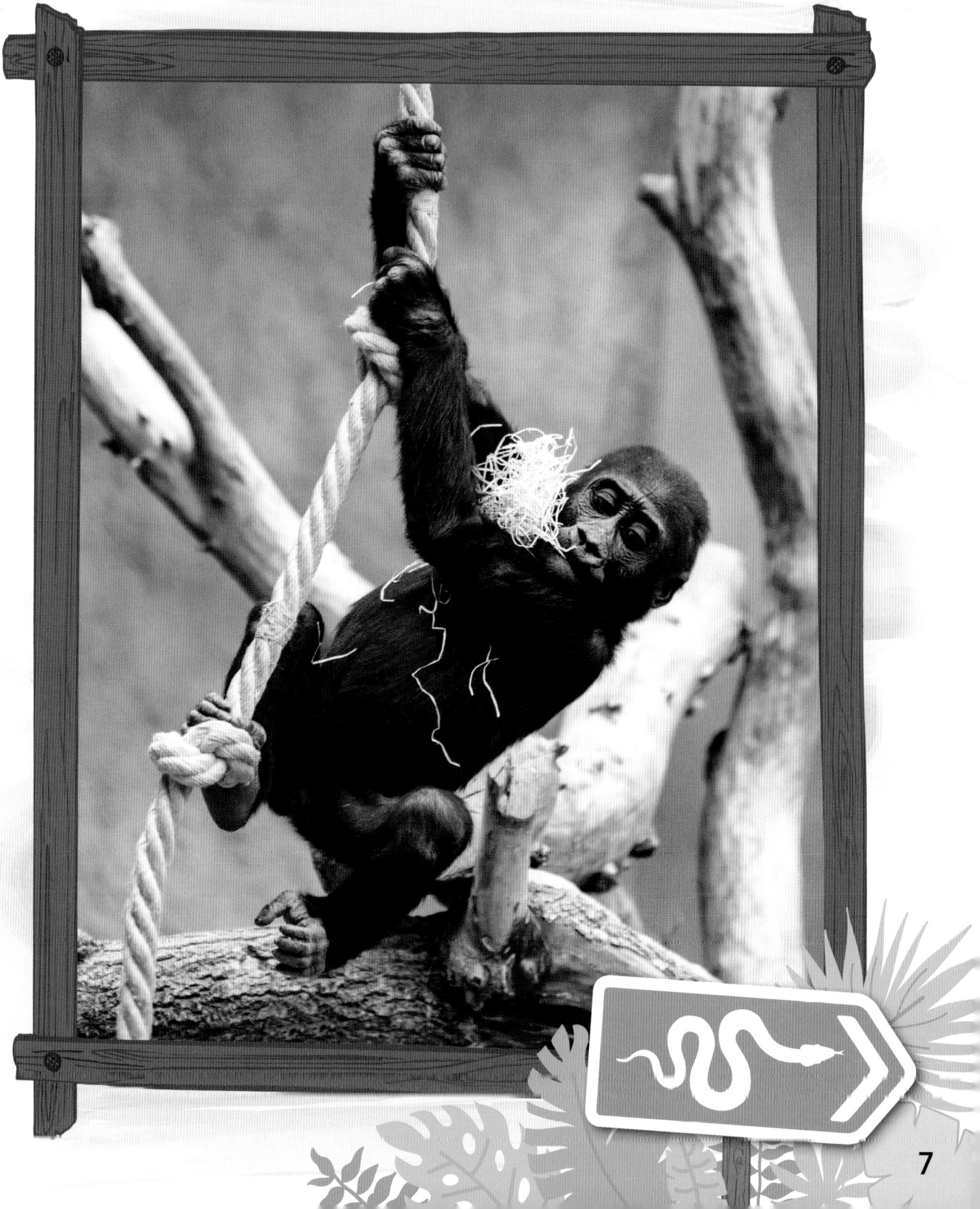

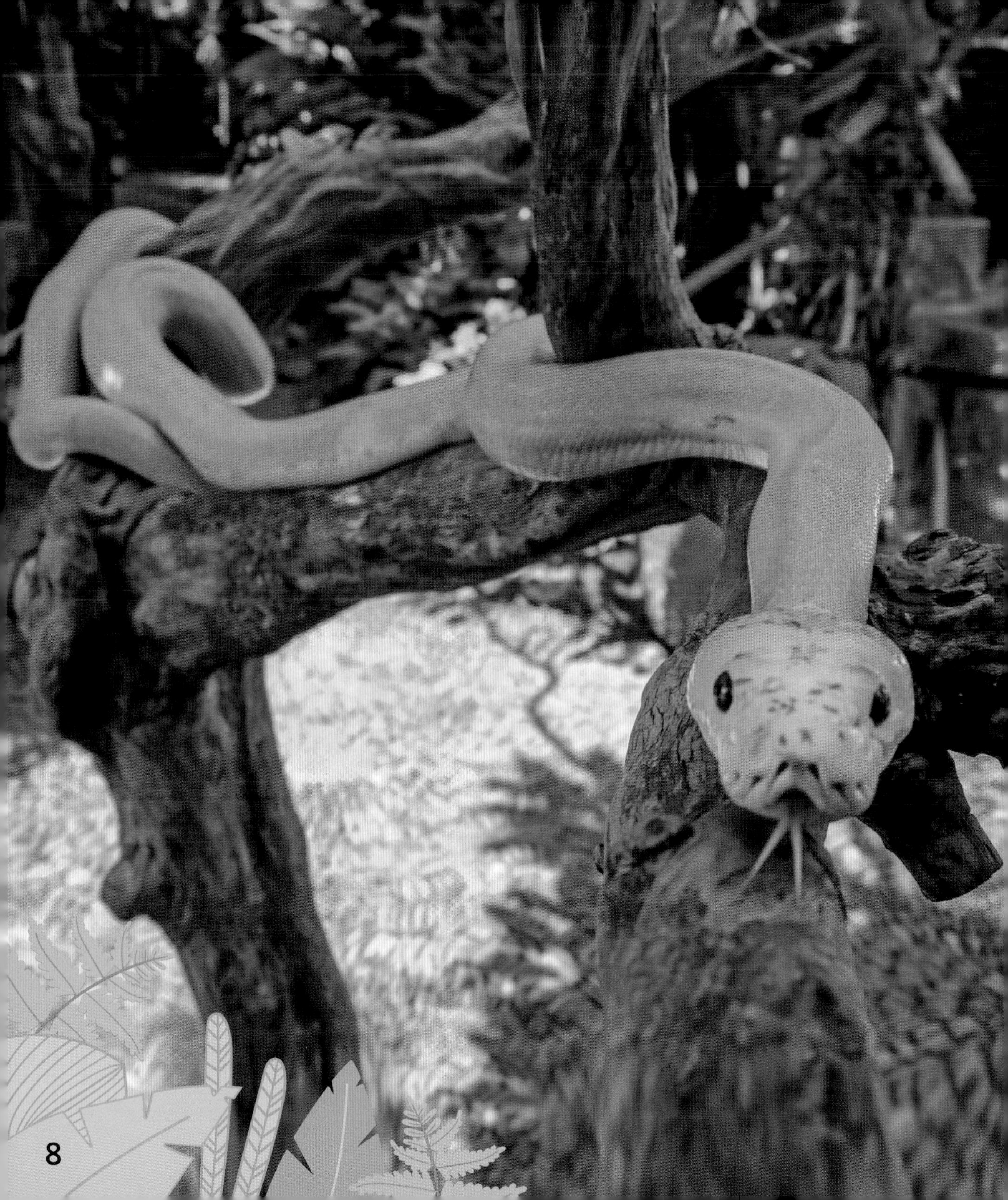

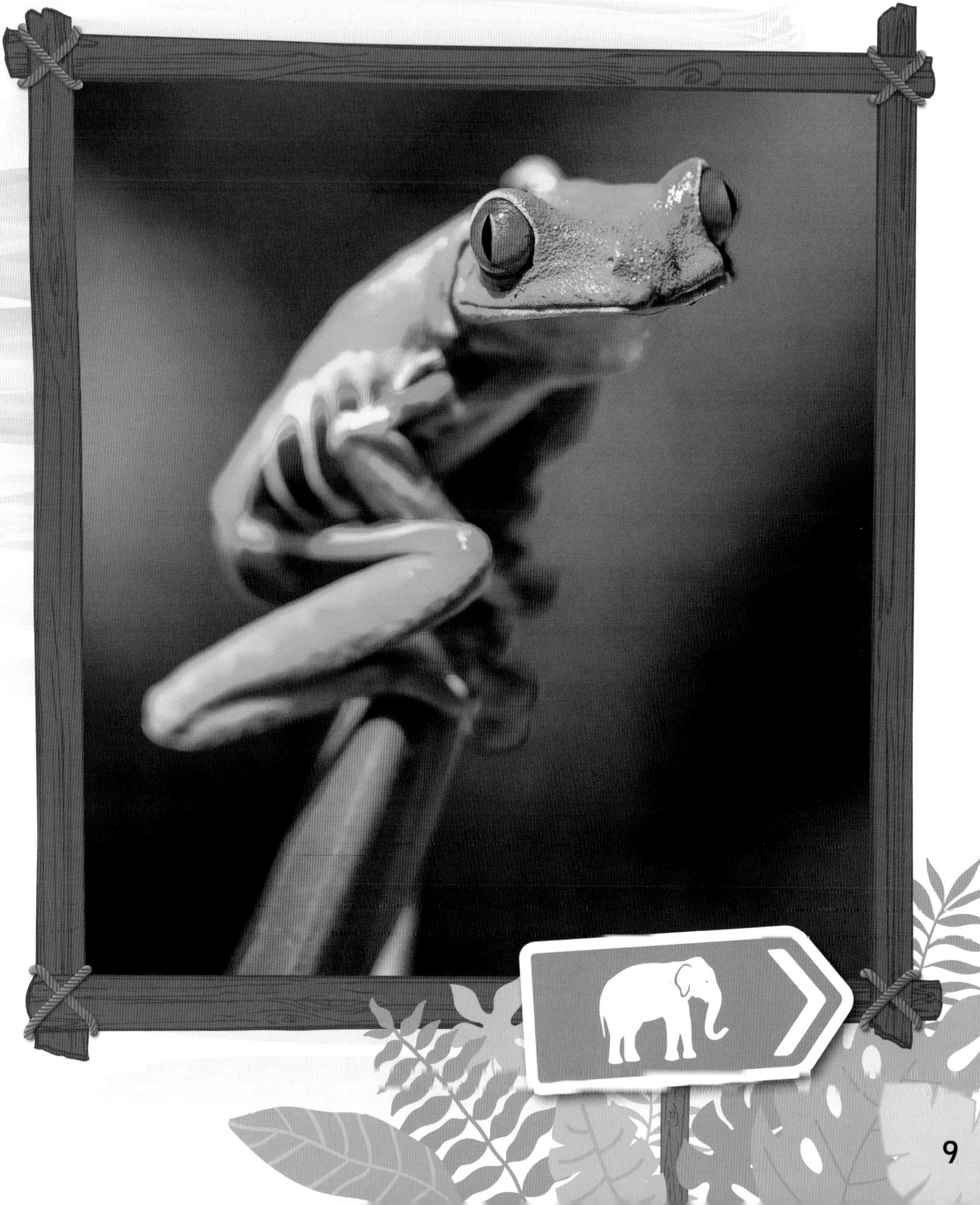

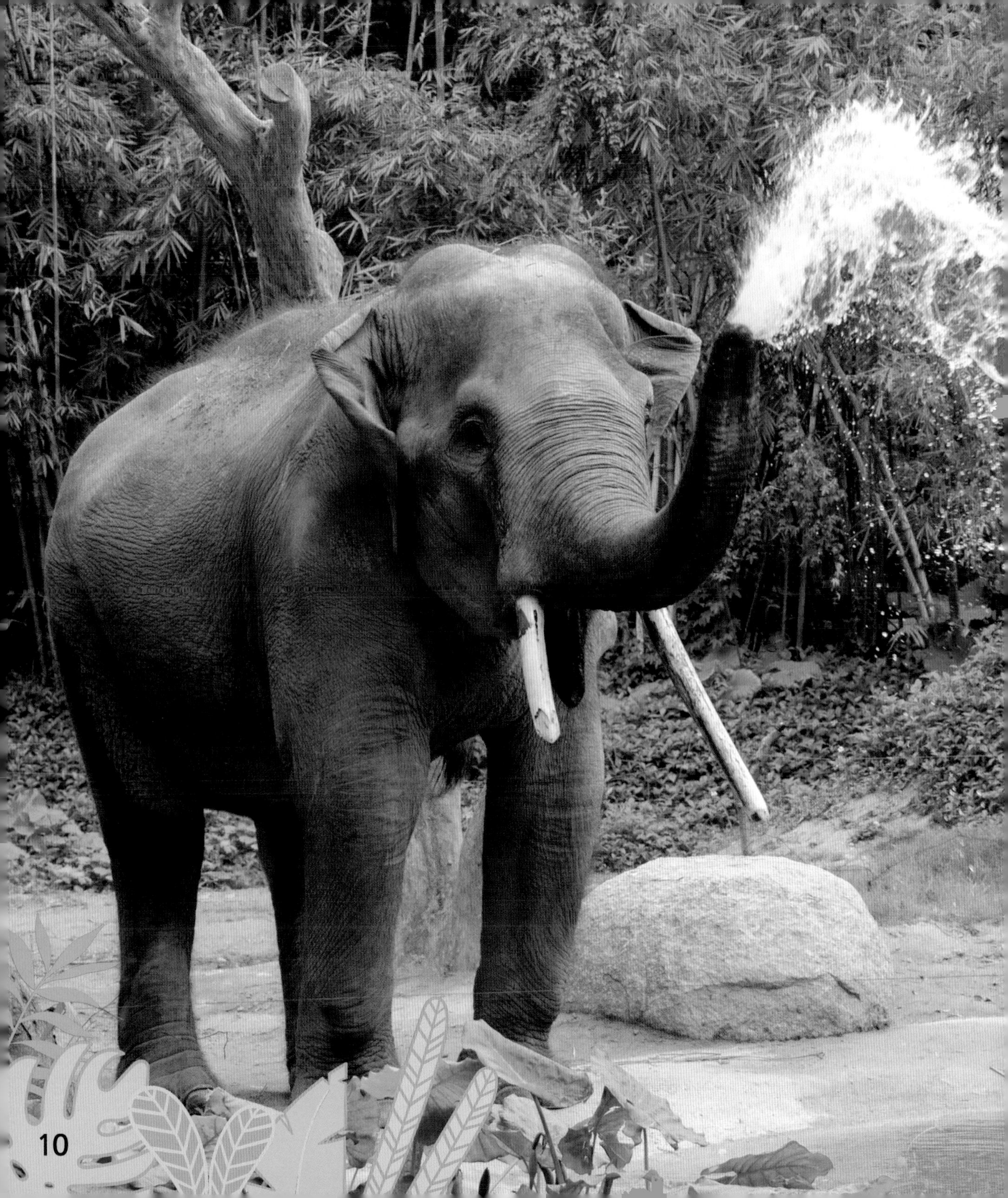

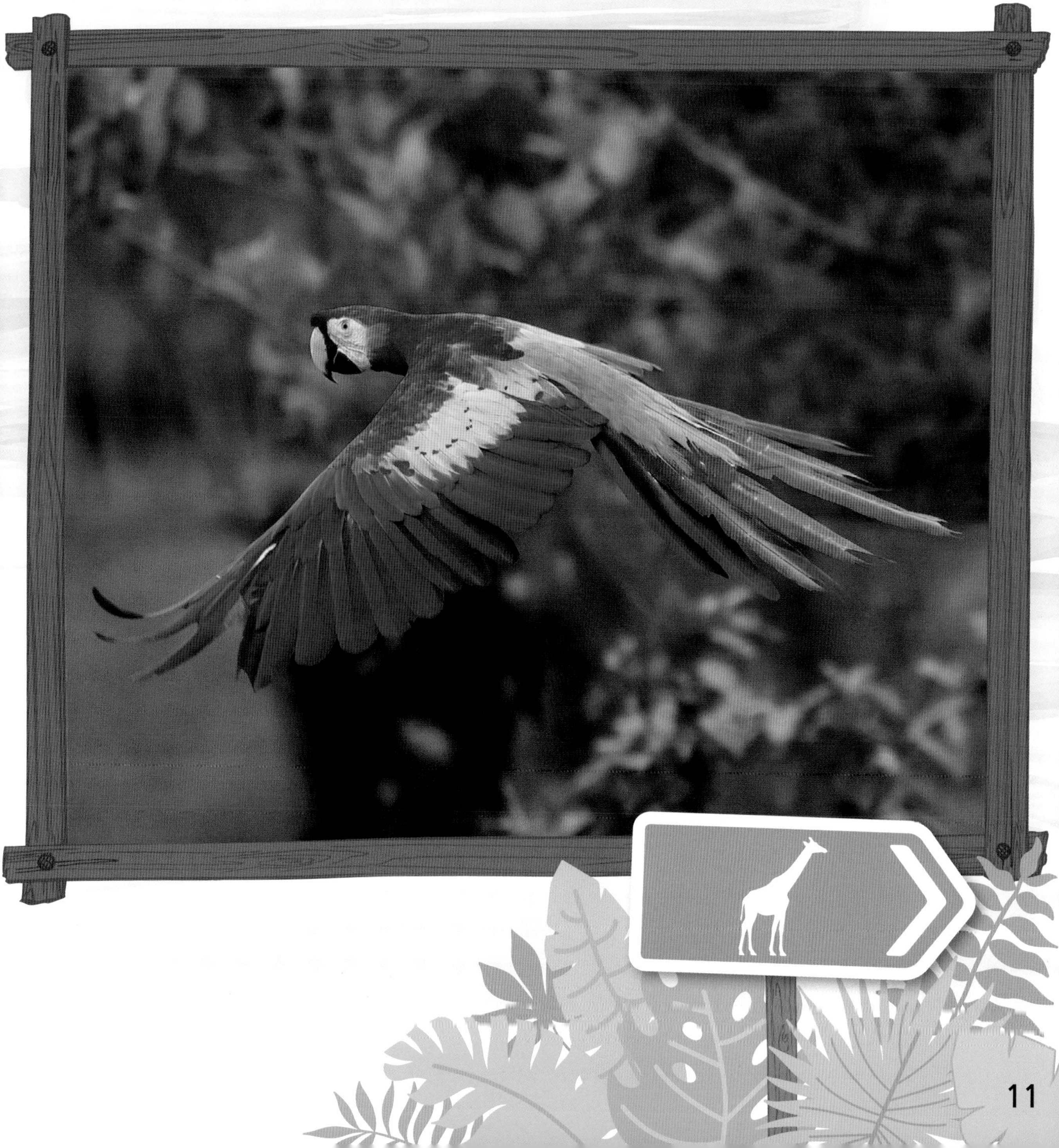

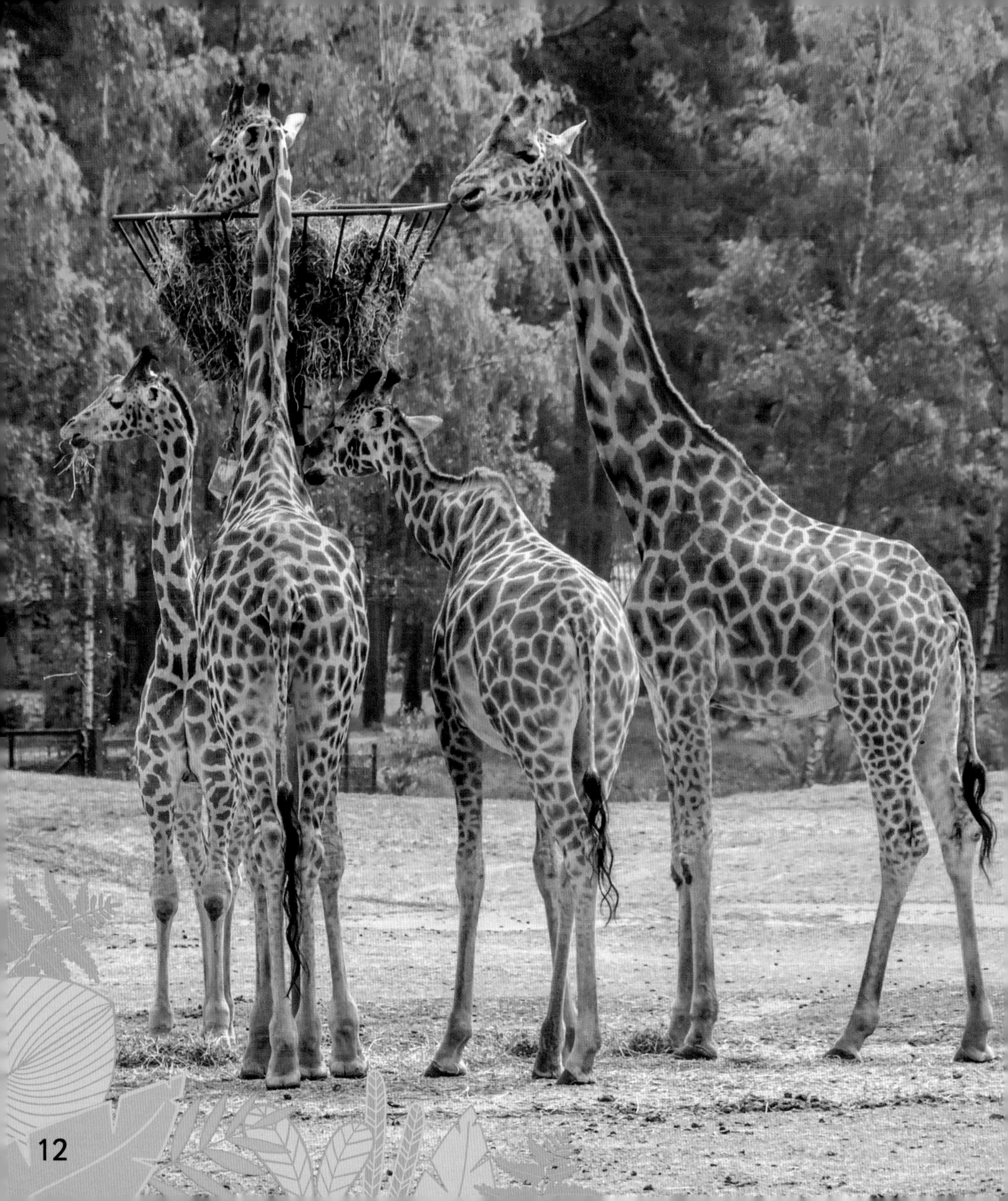